Flow
Sap

The Foremost Home Winemaking Series

General Editor **B. C. A. Turner**

Other books in the series:

Easy Guide to Home-made Wine

Simple Guide to Home-made Beer

Recipes for Home-made Wine, Mead and Beer

Making Sparkling Wines

Beer for Beginners

Making Wine once a week

Vegetable, Herb and Cereal Wines

All about Mead

Wines from Jams and Preserved Fruits

Ten types of Table Wines

Cooking with Home-made Wine and Mead

T. Edwin Belt

Flower, Leaf & Sap Wines

Mills & Boon LIMITED, LONDON
In association with
Home Beer and Wine Making

First published in Great Britain 1971 by
Mills and Boon Limited, 17–19 Foley Street, London
W1A 1DR

ISBN 0 263.51803.5

Made and printed in Great Britain by
C. Nicholls & Company Ltd
The Philips Park Press, Manchester. M11 4AU

Contents

Introduction

A Wine For Every Taste

Flower, leaf and sap wines can be made in fairly considerable variety, sufficient to satisfy every palate. The flowers, leaves and saps which are discussed within these pages, can be used for winemaking with every confidence. If you decide to experiment with other plants, do make sure that any particular part of that plant which you intend to use is not poisonous.

The amount of sugar, whether fermentable or unfermentable, which you decide to use in each recipe, will determine whether you finish up with a dry, medium or sweet wine. Flowers and leaves do not contain any natural sugar, and the weight of household sugar which is used in each recipe will determine the alcoholic strength of your wine. It is quite easy to determine the amount of natural sugar in any given volume of sap, if any, and the use of the hydrometer in this connection will be described at the appropriate time.

Flowers, leaves and saps are deficient in natural acid, and here again you are thus enabled to determine, free of complications, exactly how tart you wish your finished wine to be, since the acid content will be added by yourself.

Flowers and saps do not contain natural
tannin, and so you will also have the opportunity
to decide how much 'bite' you wish to have in
your wine. Oak and tea leaves are rich in
natural tannin.

All three of the named ingredients leave you
free to choose how much 'body' you desire
for any particular wine which is formulated
from flowers, leaves or sap, since the degree
of lightness, or of heaviness if you are looking
in that direction, will be provided by additives
to the recipe.

When making a 'heavy' as opposed to a light
wine, most people prefer rather more acid
and tannin in the formulation, since these
attributes are masked to a certain extent by
the extra body of the wine.

You can choose the alcoholic strength of
your wines by the amount of fermentable
sugar which is included in your recipe, but
only up to a maximum of about 17% alcohol
by volume (30° proof), after which, stronger
stuff can only be concocted by fortification,
which in plainer language is the straight
addition of alcohol to a finished wine; a
commercial example of this is to be found in
Port wine.

A Wine For Each Occasion

The variety of wines which we can produce
with flowers, leaves and sap is wide, and can

complement almost every dish of food. There are no hard and fast rules as to which wine should accompany any particular food, but it should be of value to learn of those formulations which have earned general acclaim for specific times of enjoyment.

A cellar of home-made wines can provide a choice of bottles from which a discriminating host may enhance each and every occasion.

The bottles of wine should be kept in a clean, adequately ventilated, dry and dark place which is not subject to extremes of temperature. A cupboard under the staircase, or a boxroom which satisfies these conditions, is all that is necessary. A constant temperature of 7–10°C (45–50°F) is ideal.

An aperitif wine is normally of 14% alcoholic strength by volume, on the sweet side of dry, with a good but not too pronounced bouquet and flavour, clean on the palate, slightly astringent, and of medium body. Such wines are intended to stimulate the appetite before a meal.

Table wines are usually the least alcoholic of wines, 10% alcohol by volume being normal. They are fairly thin in texture, light-bodied, delicate, and have a more noticeable acidity; are dry to semi-dry, and have a subtle flavour. The red wines are sometimes rich, with a touch of astringency, and the white are occasionally sweet and full-bodied; in both these cases the alcoholic strength approaches that of an aperitif. The white wines are best served at a temperature of 10°C (50°F), and the red at 18°C (64°F).

Sparkling table wines are often a little stronger, at about 12% alcohol by volume. A minor fermentation is induced in the bottle, which should be a champagne bottle if breakages are to be avoided, and the cork or stopper must be wired down. They are best served cool at about 13°C (55°F).

Social wines are appreciated at a strength around 14% alcohol by volume, semi-dry, medium flavoured and medium bodied. This is where we score over the commercial product, among which there is no comparable type of wine.

Dessert wines are those which have been fermented out to the maximum naturally obtainable strength of 17% alcohol by volume. They are at their best full-bodied, rich and sweetish, full-flavoured, and with a good bouquet; they are usually served after a meal, or with the cheese and biscuits.

Shorts or liqueurs are fortified wines, often made from wine that is strong in alcoholic content, acidity, tannin and body, but a mild-flavoured wine; this last because a distinctive flavour can then be added in the form of an essence. Sugar syrup and Polish spirit are the other ingredients used. Such wines have an alcoholic content in excess of 17% by volume. A less expensive method of making a liqueur is to freeze out some of the water from one of your own dry to dryish wines, for which you will need a deep-freezer. Liqueurs are rich, full-bodied, and of course, strong.

Aperitif wines can be made from all three of our named ingredients; flower, leaf and sap. You can buy special flavours for addition to these wines if you so wish; Vermouth is an example in the commercial field. These flavours are usually extracts of herbs, Vermouth aperitif wine being flavoured with a mixture of eight herbs. Herb flavourings are best used with a grain, flower or sap wine, as they do not blend to advantage with fruit wines.

These ingredients also lend themselves to the making of *table and social class wines,* but flowers are not always acceptable for *sweet dessert wines.*

Liqueurs can also be made from all three of the named ingredients, with the proviso that the wines used should be strong in alcoholic content, mild-flavoured, and dry to medium-dry, as mentioned above. The added flavour should, of course, complement the distinctive aroma and flavour of a flower wine.

We will be matching yeast to the type of wine which we wish to produce with each formulation, bearing in mind the suitability of the named ingredient. You can make your choice, for a start, from the following:

Aperitif wines are: dry Champagne, which is served at cellar temperature; dry and medium-dry Madeira; white Port, which is best served chilled; and dry Sherry, which is also served chilled.

Table wines are: dry Sherry, which is pale in colour and is best served with hors d'oeuvre and soup, or a medium-dry type which is full-bodied and goes well with shellfish. Dry and medium-dry Madeira to take with soup; white Burgundy to enjoy with fish; Chablis, which is a white, dry, rich and fruity Burgundy, again going well with fish; white Beaujolais, which is also a Burgundy type for complementing a dish of fish. Graves, a dry and white Bordeaux wine, excellent with shellfish; for soup, meat and game. A red, dry and light in acid Claret is served at room temperature; a red, dry and more robust wine than Claret is Burgundy, which is also served at room temperature with soup, meat and game; Hock is a fuller white wine than Moselle, and of similar character.

Sparkling table wines can be red, pink or white, and with an equally wide range of flavours. They are served chilled to slow down the effervescence.

Social wines are: a very sweet, dark-coloured and rich Sherry; a red, dry and fairly robust

Burgundy; a dry and white Bordeaux; and a sweet and full-bodied white Sauterne.

Dessert wines are: sweet Champagne, which is served at room temperature; sweet and rich Sherry; sweet, rich, full-bodied, golden-coloured Madeira; medium-dry red Port; sweet and full-bodied white Sauterne, which is the second of the best-known Bordeaux wines; and sweet Tokay.

Stocking Your Own Wine Cellar

Your wines should for preference be stored in bulk capacity containers, since they mature better in bulk rather than in individual bottles. This way they also take up less space, of course. Plastic barrels, each complete with tap, are available in two and five gallon sizes.

If, however, you produce your wines in variety, and one gallon a time, you will need half a dozen bottles for each lot. You can buy the bottles if you prefer to do so, but a friendly wine waiter at a licensed restaurant, or publican will no doubt be delighted if you cart away his empties.

The traditionalists always use new corks for their bottles, but plastic stoppers can also be bought from your home-winemaking supplier, and these can be used again. Corked bottles must be stored on their sides, in order to keep the corks moist, airtight and well-fitting; a wine-bottle rack is almost a necessity in such circumstances. If you use plastic stoppers, make sure that they are a good fit; their advantage is that the bottles can be stored standing upright on suitable shelving, and thus probably take up less room. Plastic bottle closures give a professional finish to your corked bottles, and bottle labels are also available to this end. It is desirable to invest in a corking machine, and these are available in varying degrees of sophistication according to the price which you are prepared to pay. A good bottle-opener is perhaps even more desirable – there is a type on the market which, if known to everyone, must make all other designs redundant. It comprises an automatically self-centering corkscrew combined with an unscrewing device which lifts out the cork without any strain on your muscles whatsoever, and makes a clean job of it every time.

1 How to make Quality Wines

The Essential Ingredients

The first requirement of a wine is that it must have an alcoholic content. Yeast and sugar are the ingredients used in formulations for the production of alcohol. The second requirement is that the yeast must be provided with sustenance to enable it to function to its full capacity. Nutrient salts are added, when necessary, for this purpose. There must be a degree of acidity, and this is provided, when absent, by citric, malic or tartaric acids. Tannin is required to give a wine a slight astringency and bite. Flavour and aroma are imparted by a bulk ingredient after which the wine is usually named. The amount of alcohol, unfermented sugar, acid, tannin and flavour, together with the density of the wine, all combine to give it body, without which it would be thin and watery.

A quality wine is the outcome when all these ingredients are present in the correct quantities and proportions.

We will later discuss how this is to be achieved in the case of each of our three classes of wine; flower, leaf and sap. Before doing this, however, let us consider the yeasts, sugars, and other essential ingredients which are available.

Yeast can be purchased in the form of baker's,
brewer's, granulated, tablet, powder, paste,
and liquid, together with varieties grown on
agar jelly, and some from Germany on dried
rosehip. Yeasts specifically produced for use
in winemaking are generally available in tablet
and liquid form, and these are the products we
shall be describing in the following recipes.
Baker's yeast produces a rapid fermentation,
which is not always desirable in winemaking,
and it is not to be recommended for wines
intended to have a high alcoholic content; it
can also cause off-flavours if left in contact
with the rudimentary wine for too long. These
same remarks can be applied to brewer's
yeast, and in addition it can give a bitter
residual hop flavour to your wine. The others
can be experimented with at your leisure, and
on inclination, but we will confine ourselves
to specific wine yeasts in these pages, and in
particular to the tablet forms. Some liquid
and tablet wine yeasts have the advantage
that they can be added direct to the must
(this is the mixture awaiting the addition of
the yeast; all prepared ready for fermentation
into wine). Other liquid and tablet wine yeasts
have to be prepared at least forty-eight hours
before they are required for use, with the aid
of a 'starter' solution, for which the required
ingredients can be:

$\frac{1}{2}$ oz (14g) Malt extract
$\frac{1}{16}$ oz (2g) Citric acid
$\frac{1}{4}$ oz (7g) Sugar
$\frac{1}{2}$ pint (0.25 litres) Water

These particular ingredients have been chosen because they are the stock in trade of the home-winemaker and brewer. You could, if you so wished, use fruit juice and sugar, sultanas and sugar, or any similar complete yeast food which will reactivate the yeast.

Tablet wine yeast is being made available in ever increasing selection, but a good foundation of types prior to experimentation on your own account is as follows:

Aperitif: Sherry, Madeira, Champagne, Port.
Table: Sherry, Madeira, Burgundy, Chablis, Beaujolais, Graves, Bordeaux, Hock.
Sparkling Table: Champagne.
Social: Sherry, Burgundy, Bordeaux, Sauterne.
Dessert: Champagne, Sherry, Madeira, Port, Bordeaux, Tokay, Sauterne.

A good 'general purpose' yeast will often be our choice within these pages, since the wines to be made from flowers, leaves and sap are unique, and do not readily fall within commercial wine categories. The yeasts mentioned will not produce a wine of their stated name from our ingredients. They will, however, bring out the natural flavour of a similar formulation, and even more important, they will give you the best opportunity of producing a wine of 17% alcoholic content by volume, which is the most you can hope for from the fermentation process. They also throw a firm sediment, and do not readily impart off-flavours. Stronger wines in the 'shorts' class are produced by the addition of Polish spirit, and you must be sure to increase the other attributes of the wine when formulating it, in order to maintain a correct balance with the alcohol, as has previously been mentioned when we described 'body' as applied to wine.

The amount of yeast to use in any given volume of must, is not critical. A good, adequate and steady fermentation cannot be expected if too small an amount of yeast is used, since it will take time to multiply itself into a sufficient labour force. On the other hand, too great a surplus of yeast will increase the chance of the development of off-flavours. The tablet form is generally used at the rate of one per gallon (5 litres); baker's and brewer's yeast at one ounce (30 grammes) per gallon; the granulated type at one teaspoonful per gallon. When yeast is to be prepared in a starter solution, and the quantity of yeast supplied is said to be sufficient for, say 5 gallons, (22.5 litres), it is advisable to use it all in the starter, and then divide the starter into smaller fractions of not less than one third per gallon.

Ordinary household granulated white sugar (sucrose) is eminently suitable for our purpose. Invert sugar can be used if you so wish, but it costs more and only enables the fermentation process to start a little sooner.

Some ingredients contain natural sugar, which will be taken into account in our recipes.

Nutrient salts can be bought in tablet and powder form, and then should be used as directed by the manufacturer. We will describe the requirements from these salts, since they will help us to understand the build-up of our formulations. Amino acids are a constituent of cereals, fruits and roots, and at least one type of such produce must form a part of other wine formulations, since these acids are a nutrient requirement. Our standard further requirement in nutrient salts is ammonium phosphate, which is used at the rate of one teaspoonful per gallon. You may like to try the addition of a 3 mg size vitamin B_1 tablet (Benerva tablet) per gallon of the wines described herein, and indeed we will include it in the recipes, thus keeping the yeast healthy and active.

Citric, malic and tartaric acids, when not present in the ingredients of our must as a complete trio, have to be augmented by any one, two, or all three as the case may be. Citric acid is present in lemons, and eight of these fruit are equivalent to one ounce of the crystals purchased over the counter at your chemist or home-winemaking shop. These acids are needed so as to ensure good growing conditions for the yeast, and to improve the keeping quality of your finished wine. They are required in the must, either as a natural constituent or as an additive, in the

proportions of 1:2:2 citric, malic, tartaric
respectively. Sweet wines require a little
more, say half as much acid again than dry
wines.

Tannin assists in the clearing and maturation
of wine. It is present in some produce which
we use for winemaking, sometimes to a very
considerable extent, but generally speaking it
is conspicuous by its absence, which is very
noticeable in a finished wine. It is available
as grape tannin solution from the suppliers
of home-winemaking ingredients, and is
otherwise obtained in the form of a few oak
leaves or pear peelings added to the must. It
is the more readily provided in the form of
half a teaspoonful of tea to the gallon of wine
being produced, in those cases where it is
entirely absent from the natural ingredients,
but somewhat less for light wines. I prefer to
scald a teabag with a pint of water, and leave
it to brew and to cool, after which half this
amount is used for each gallon of must. This
way there is no trouble with the tea leaves, of
course, which can be removed intact in their
bag from the jug or other container in which
the tea has been brewed.

Raisins and sultanas should be mentioned as
generally improving the quality of the wines
under discussion.

We will now decide upon the general
requirements for the formulation of flower,
leaf and sap wines, in the light of these facts,

and in consideration of their natural
constituents.

Using Flowers
Flowers leave the winemaker free to arrange
the alcoholic strength of his or her wines
quite simply by the amount of sugar which is
added, since flowers do not provide this
ingredient, although the 'body' additive may
contain natural sugar, and this must be
allowed for in our formulations.

Amino acids are present in root vegetables,
cereals, malt, fresh or dried fruit, and one or
more of these ingredients will be included in
our flower wine formulations as a source of
amino acid.

Ammonium phosphate will also have to be
provided, the quantity being two teaspoonfuls
per gallon.

Citric, malic and tartaric acids must be
included in our formulations, and the
quantities are upwards of $\frac{1}{8}$, $\frac{1}{4}$ and $\frac{1}{4}$ of a
teaspoonful respectively.

The tannin content of flowers can be ignored,
and this ingredient will be included in our
flower wine formulations in the form of $\frac{1}{4}$–$\frac{1}{2}$ a
teaspoonful of tea leaves per gallon of must,
prepared as described on page 20.

It will be seen that the only contribution to
our recipes which can be provided by flowers

is in their bouquet and flavour. Hence we must
also include an ingredient to provide the
'body' in our flower wines. This will normally
be available from the product or products
which are included for their amino acid content,
and we will arrange matters so that this is
invariably so; in other words, we will choose
our source of 'body' from the amino acid
containing products mentioned above.
Generally speaking, half a gallon of flower
heads or petals will provide all the flavour
and bouquet which we need in the flower
wines, and in particular, you will be well
advised to reduce this amount to a pint in the
case of the elderflower and golden rod. The
product used for providing body must not
mask the attributes of the flower, of course,
otherwise we will not be making a flower wine.

Flowers are dried for storage and marketing
purposes, of course, and you will need two
ounces of the dried flowers for each quart of
fresh flowers given in a recipe. Alternatively,
dried flowers are, on average, one eighth of
their weight when gathered fresh.

A sweet flower wine should have rather more
flavour. Social wines are those most likely to
be appreciated when flowers are employed in
their making, and particularly when they are
semi-sweet.

Using Leaves
Leaves are chiefly a source of flavour for wine,
with some bouquet. All the other

requirements for a balanced must, except
tannin, have to be provided in the
formulation, although there are exceptions to
this general rule.

Hence the alcoholic strength of leaf wines is
determined solely by the amount of sugar
which we use, other things being equal, and
up to a maximum of 17% alcohol by volume.

Amino acids will be provided in the form of a
root vegetable, a fruit or a cereal, malt or a
dried fruit.

Ammonium phosphate is an essential additive,
to the extent of two teaspoonfuls per gallon.

Acid is normally required in the proportions of
$\frac{1}{8}$ of a teaspoonful of citric, $\frac{1}{4}$ of a teaspoonful
of malic, and $\frac{1}{4}$ of a teaspoonful of tartaric,
upwards, per gallon in all leaf wines.

In the comparatively rare instances when the
leaf used does not contain tannin, we will be
using $\frac{1}{2}$ a teaspoonful of tea leaves, prepared
as previously described, added to each gallon
of must.

Body has to be provided, and is usually
available in the amino acid additive, but do
not use potatoes for this purpose as they give
harshness to a wine – bananas are very good.
An advantage of bananas is that they do not
provide an over-riding flavour of their own,
unless used in excess, in which case we would

be producing a banana wine, and the leaves
would serve no good purpose, since their
flavour would be hidden.

You may wish to dry some leaves for future
use, and if you do so, it will be helpful if you
weigh them before and after dehydration, and
especially so if the fresh weight is related to,
say, a quart of the leaves, or to any other
convenient volume. A quart of fresh leaves will
dehydrate to two ounces in weight.

Using Sap

Some trees produce a sap rich in sugar; such
a tree is the maple. It is a comparatively simple
matter to determine the amount of sugar
contained in a gallon of sap. This is achieved
by the use of a hydrometer, as will be
explained later. In the absence of natural
sugar in the sap, the strength of your wine will
be determined solely by the amount of sugar
which you use in the formulation.

Amino acids must be added to the saps
which are commonly used for winemaking,
and raisins are a good source of these. They
also provide body.

Sap musts should be provided with one
teaspoonful per gallon of ammonium
phosphate.

Acids should be added in the proportions of
$\frac{1}{8}-\frac{1}{4}$ of a teaspoonful of citric, and $\frac{1}{4}-\frac{1}{2}$ of a
teaspoonful each of malic and tartaric acids,

upwards, per gallon, since saps are deficient in acid.

Tannin is usually needed in white wines, and you should add half a teaspoonful of tea leaves, prepared as described on page 20, to each gallon of must. In the unexpected event of your wine then having too much bite, this can be rectified by the means of gelatine. No more, and preferably less than $\frac{1}{8}$ of a teaspoonful of pure gelatine, such as that used in the production of jelly, is soaked in half an eggcupful of previously boiled cold water, after which previously boiled hot water is added and stirred in until the gelatine has been dissolved. The cooled mixture is then stirred well into the wine.

Now that the general principles to be followed in the formulation of your wines has been made clear, the general principles to be followed in the method of production of quality wines can be discussed.

The Method

Principles
Sterilization of all equipment is the first essential. This is effected by a thorough rinsing with a solution made up of $1\frac{1}{2}$ oz (50 grammes) of sodium metabisulphite and 4 oz (125 grammes) of citric acid per gallon (5 litres) of water. Allow the equipment, which will include your wine bottles, to drip-dry.

Sterilization of ingredients is equally important. Whenever boiling water is used, this answers the purpose. However, the collection of sap sufficient to make a gallon of wine can take a few days, and it is advisable to sterilize each day's collection by the addition of Campden tablets at the rate of three to the gallon.

The type of wine which you intend to make will determine the amount of sugar which is required in the must. Flowers and leaves are devoid of natural sugar content, and so are some saps, in which case the required sugar content when using such ingredients is as follows:

		per gallon	per 5 litres
10% alcohol by volume =	2 lb 0 oz	1.00 kg
12% „ „ „ =	2 lb 8 oz	1.20 kg
14% „ „ „ =	2 lb 12 oz	1.40 kg
17% „ „ „ =	3 lb 4 oz	1.65 kg

When the sap has a natural sugar content, it is necessary to find out how much sugar will have to be added to the must in order to bring it up to these concentrations. It will be appreciated that sap varies in its sugar content from one species of tree to another, and between trees of the same species, also from one season to another, so we cannot be precise in this respect without a test to determine the sugar content.

To determine the amount of natural sugar in

the must, we use a hydrometer floated in a hydrometer jar containing a sample of the sap. The specific gravity reading which is thereby obtained, is related to the sugar content of the sap, and in accordance with the accompanying Alcoholic Strength Chart, which also gives the amount of sugar to be added for each type of wine.

Our aim is to ferment to dryness (change all the sugar into alcohol), and medium to sweet wines will be obtained by the addition of lactose, a non-fermentable sugar. A convenient time to add the lactose is when filling the storage containers (jars, barrels or bottles), or when filling the decanter, since it is the modern practice to decant all wines, white as well as red. The lactose is added, dissolved in the minimum volume of water or wine, in the proportion of $\frac{1}{2}$ to 4 oz per gallon (15 to 125 grammes per 5 litres) of wine, according to the sweetness required, and either more or less according to the heaviness of the finished wine.

Wines containing up to 14% alcohol by volume will normally ferment out to dryness, given a suitable formulation and a correct method, but stronger wines will repay special attention. The weight of sugar required to be fermented will be 3 lb 4 oz in one gallon of must. The procedure to be adopted, assuming that the ingredients contain no natural sugar, is as follows: dissolve $1\frac{1}{2}$ lb sugar in one pint of water, bringing briefly to the boil, and add to the must, topping up with boiled water to the six pint mark. Fermentation is allowed to proceed for four days, stirring three times a day, after which the solids are strained off, and the liquid pressed out of them, into a fermentation jar fitted with an airlock. When this fermentation has slowed down (after about a further three days – specific gravity 1.010), half of the rest of the sugar is added, but only after it has been dissolved in one pint of water as described above. After the ferment has slowed down once more, the vessel is topped up to the one gallon mark with the remainder of the sugar in solution. Racking is carried out after seven days, then after a further fourteen days, and the syphon is made to deliver into a funnel, so that a cascade into the fermentation jar occurs. Thereafter rack monthly in the same manner, and until fermentation is complete.

The degree of acidity required in our wines is measured in pH units. The neutral point between acidity/alkalinity is pH7. Hence the lower the pH value under 7, the greater is the degree of acidity. In the stronger wines in particular, we must provide good living conditions for the yeast if it is not to be inhibited and leave us with a weaker (and sweetish rather than dry) wine than that which it is our intention to produce. The pH value which we seek in this respect is 3.3, with an allowance of 0.1 either way. There are acid-testing kits on the home-winemaking market which come with full instructions for their use, and consequently there is no need to elaborate further on this subject, except to mention that precipitated chalk will reduce acid content, and citric acid is most suitable for increasing the acid content.

It has been mentioned that flowers, leaves and saps do not provide the required body to wines in which the flower, leaf or sap is the characteristic ingredient. This body may be provided by the addition to your formulations of vegetables, cereals, malt extract, dried or fresh fruit, in accordance with the following table of the amount of each ingredient required for one gallon of the given wine.

	Vegetable	Cereal	Malt Extract	Dried Fruit	Fresh Fruit
Aperitif	16 oz	14 oz	8 oz	14 oz	20 oz
Table Sparkling	12 oz	12 oz	6 oz	12 oz	12 oz
Table	16 oz	14 oz	8 oz	14 oz	20 oz
Social	20 oz	16 oz	10 oz	16 oz	28 oz
Dessert	28 oz	20 oz	14 oz	20 oz	36 oz

If you decide to experiment with the use of more than one of these ingredients in any one particular wine, then they should be used proportionately. For instance, if you wish to try a Social wine made with 14 oz of bananas (fresh fruit), then if your other ingredient is sultanas (dried fruit), you will need 8 oz of it. These fruits have been chosen as an example because they are very suitable for providing the body in the wines now under discussion.

They will not mask the delicate bouquet and flavour of flower wines.

You may be aware that fresh fruit dries to approximately one quarter of its fresh weight, and the above table needs some explanation. The weights given for dried fruits are for the commonly used dates, figs, raisins, sultanas, and currants, which demand a fresh fruit weight of four times their given dried fruit weight, as opposed to the fresh fruit weights for all other fruits given in the fresh fruit table.

Dates, figs, raisins, sultanas and currants contain up to half their dry weight in sugar, and malt extract contains up to three-quarters its syrup weight in sugar. Use your hydrometer to ascertain the specific gravity of the must, and add the weight of sugar shown opposite this figure under the required wine.

Rohament P must be mentioned in connection with the body of flower, leaf and sap wines, since it will pulp the produce used to provide that body, and without the loss of vitamins; this without boiling. It should be used in conjunction with Pectinol if the body-providing produce contains pectin, and with the acid which is required for the formulation of the wine. The Rohament P and the Pectinol are each used in the proportion of one teaspoonful to 5 lb of produce. The procedure is to stir the powders into the water in which the produce is immersed, leave at room temperature for twenty-four hours, and then heat up to, at the least, 66°C (151°F), and press out the juice while still hot. A standard thermostatically

Alcoholic Strength Chart

Specific Gravity of must at 21°C (70°F)	Ounces of additional sugar to be included in one gallon of must to increase potential alcoholic content to 10, 12, or 14% by volume			Sugar to be included in 6 pints of must to increase initial potential alcoholic content to 10% for 17% wines
	10%	12%	14%	
1.015	27	34	40	20
1.020	24	31	37	18
1.025	22	29	35	16
1.030	19	26	32	14
1.035	16	23	29	12
1.040	14	21	27	10
1.045	12	19	25	9
1.050	10	17	23	7
1.055	8	15	21	6
1.060	6	13	19	4
1.065	4	11	17	3
1.070	2	9	15	1
1.075		7	13	
1.080		5	11	
1.085		2	8	
1.090			6	
1.095			4	
1.100			2	

controlled electric immersion heater of the
type used for mashing in the production of
beer at home makes this process quite simple,
but no harm will be done if you bring the
liquid briefly to boiling point.

It will be appreciated that metal, which is
subject to attack by acids, or lead glazed
vessels, must not be used in this or other
winemaking processes in which acids are
involved. Aluminium, stainless steel, and
plastic vessels are readily obtainable, and are
acid-resistant.

When delicate aromas and flavours are
involved, it is generally advantageous to use
the cold water method of extraction. Campden
tablets can be employed to ensure the
sterility of the must.

Yeast is killed at temperatures in excess of
38°C (100°F), and it is important, therefore, to
allow musts which have been prepared by
extraction and by sterilization by heat, to cool
to 21°C (70°F) before adding the yeast or yeast
starter. This is the best temperature at which
to keep the yeast active in its work of primary
fermentation, and fluctuations in temperature
should be avoided. Secondary fermentations
are best carried on at 18°C (64°F). At 7°C
(45°F) most wine yeasts cease to function,
and they can be kept in a dormant state in the
refrigerator until required for use. Fermentation
in the bottle for the production of sparkling
table wine should be arranged at a

temperature of 13°C (55°F). Tokay is an exceptional yeast in that it works best at a temperature of 33°C (91°F), and with such effectiveness that its work is normally completed within a fortnight.

All the ingredients except the yeast, are brought to the boil in the water, and simmered for five minutes, when preparing a yeast starter. The yeast is added when the mixture has cooled to 21°C (70°F).

Do not fail to store your red wines in brown or green coloured bottles. Keep the light away from them by this or other means when storing in bulk, otherwise they will lose their colour. The fermentation jar should also be kept protected from daylight.

The principles involved in making liqueurs, do not fall within the practice of wine-making, but are more of an adjunct. Any wine with a high alcoholic content, of good body, and of weak flavour, can be used for this purpose. A wine from which the flowers or leaves have been omitted will serve our purpose admirably, provided the other attributes have been increased accordingly; the body, in particular, should be three times the weight stated in the table on page 29.

Added ingredients are Polish spirit, sugar, and a flavouring essence. Vodka is the same as Polish spirit. The spirit is available at 100° and 140° proof. Choose a liqueur to make

from those which bear some resemblance to
the wine being used, if only in colour. Your
wine preferably will be 30° proof (17% alcohol
by volume).

A spirit bottle contains 755 cc (26.6 fl. oz). Put
one teaspoonful, or 3 cc ($\frac{1}{8}$ fl. oz) of the
flavouring essence into the bottle, followed by
175 cc (6 fl. oz) of cold sugar syrup; this last
coming from your stock solution of 2 lb (900
grammes) sugar dissolved to boiling point in
600 cc (1 pint) of water. Now add the amount
of spirit which is required to give your
chosen strength of liqueur, and in accordance
with the accompanying Degrees Proof Chart;
then top up with wine. Cork, shake to mix,
and you can get out your liqueur glasses a
week later. This will form a basis for future
experimentation to suit your own taste. If the
bottle of flavouring essence carries instructions
for the amount of essence to use, follow
those instructions, of course – the
manufacturer knows the strength of his
products better than his new customers – you
can then experiment to suit your own taste.

Degrees Proof Chart
To fortify 30° proof wine with 100° or 140°
proof Polish spirit: for the desired alcoholic
strength of your liqueur, use spirit to the
amount given below: per 755 cc (26.6 fl. oz)
bottle. It is obviously more accurate to use
metric measures, and a hydrometer jar can be
obtained which is calibrated in cubic
centimetres, thus serving a dual purpose.

Liqueur strength	100° proof spirit	140° proof spirit
40° proof;	80cc (3 fl. oz)	50cc (2 fl. oz)
" 50° "	160cc (6 fl. oz)	100cc (4 fl. oz)
" 60° "	250cc (9 fl. oz)	150cc (5 fl. oz)
" 70° "	330cc (11 fl. oz)	200cc (7 fl. oz)

Practice

All Wines Except Dessert

1   All the equipment to be used is sterilized by a thorough rinsing in the sulphite and acid solution, followed by drip-drying.

2   Leaves should be washed in cold running water.

3a   For flower and leaf wines, pour boiling water into a plastic bucket containing the main ingredients and the sugar, stirring to dissolve the sugar.

3b   Alternatively for flower and leaf wines, of delicate scent and/or flavour, pour tapwater into a plastic bucket containing the main ingredients, stir in three crushed Campden tablets, and leave covered with linen sheet for twenty-four hours. Then dissolve the sugar in boiling water, and add to the contents of the bucket.

3c   For sap wines, simmer the sap for fifteen minutes in an aluminium pan, stirring in the sugar after ten minutes, and pour onto the main ingredient(s) contained in a plastic bucket.

4   Make up to the one gallon (5 litre) mark with boiled water in the case of flower and leaf wines. Add the acids and the tannin ($\frac{1}{2}$ pint of tea), using all or none, according to the natural constituents of the main ingredients,

and stir with a plastic spoon to dissolve the
chemicals. Allow to cool to 21°C (70°F),
keeping covered with linen sheeting. Take a
hydrometer reading if the main ingredients
contain sugar – adjust the sugar content if
necessary, using the Alcoholic Strength Chart.

5   Stir in the ammonium phosphate, vitamin
B1 tablet, and the yeast. If a yeast starter is
being used, this should have been prepared
forty-eight hours previously. Cover with linen
sheeting to let the air in and to keep the
vinegar fly out.

6   Leave this primary aerobic fermentation
in progress for three days for 10%, five days
for 12%, and seven days for 14% (alcohol by
volume) wines, keeping a steady temperature
of 21°C (70°F) for white wines, and 24°C
(75°F) for rich red wines – this last with the
use of an electric thermostatically controlled
immersion heater such as is used in the
home-brewing of beer. Do not exceed these
temperatures, but if the must is merely kept at
room temperature it will come to no harm. Stir
thrice daily – this is important in the case of
flower and leaf wines, so that they do not dry
out in a 'crust' on the surface.

7   Strain the liquid through muslin, nylon,
or plastic mesh into another bucket, allow to
settle, after which, syphon into a
fermentation jar, top up to the neck with
boiled and cooled water, if required, and fit

the cork and fermentation lock. Keep at 18°C (64°F), or at room temperature, for this secondary anaerobic fermentation.

8   Rack (syphon off from the lees or solids at the bottom of the jar) after a month. Top up the liquid in the jar as before. It is just possible that fermentation will now have ceased (no more bubbles through the fermentation lock), but it can proceed for many more weeks. Keep the end of the syphon tube at the bottom of the container which is being filled, so as to minimize the absorption of oxygen. If making a sparkling table wine, save some of the yeast deposit in a small bottle in the refrigerator.

9   Rack again after a further month if fermentation is still proceeding. The top of the receiving vessel must be, of course, at a lower level than the bottom of the discharging vessel. The syphon is started by sucking on the discharge end of the tube. Do not allow the other end of the clear plastic tube to disturb the sediment in the discharging vessel – a glass U-bend is a help in this respect. Top up with cool, previously boiled water.

10   Rack again after a month, if bubbling has not ceased before. You can now replace the fermentation lock by a small square of polythene wrapping material secured by a rubber band, or preferably by one of the patent stoppers with a ball-bearing release valve which are on the market. In the event of

any further sedimentation, rack again. Top up
as before.

11   Bottle, or syphon into bulk containers
after a total wine-making time of six months,
and store at a temperature of about 7–10°C
(45–50°F). If making a sparkling table wine,
make a yeast starter bottle from the
refrigerated yeast at least three days before
bottling, and add a teaspoonful of this starter,
together with a teaspoonful of sugar, to each
champagne bottle, and wire down.
Champagne bottles must be used – wine
bottles will burst under the considerable
pressure of the carbon dioxide gas which
provides the effervescence in this wine. Add
lactose solution for 'sweeter than dry' wines,
as has been described previously.

Dessert Wines
1   Sterilize all equipment as described.
2   Wash leaves in cold running water.

3a   For flower and leaf wines, pour four pints
of boiling water into a plastic bucket
containing the main ingredients and half the
total weight of sugar to be used; stir to
dissolve the sugar.

3b   Alternatively for flower and leaf wines,
pour three pints of tapwater into a plastic
bucket containing the main ingredients, stir
in a crushed Campden tablet, and leave
covered with linen sheeting for twenty-four
hours. Then dissolve half of the total weight

of sugar to be used in a pint of boiling water, and add to the contents of the bucket.

3c   For sap wines, simmer half of the sap for fifteen minutes in an aluminium pan, stirring in half of the total weight of sugar after ten minutes, and pour onto the main ingredient(s) contained in a plastic bucket.

4   Add the acids and the tannin (half a pint of tea), using all or none according to the natural constituents of the main ingredients, and stir with a plastic spoon to dissolve the chemicals. Make up only to the six pint mark with boiled water; with boiled sap in the case of sap wines. Allow to cool to 21°C (70°F), keeping covered with linen sheeting. Take a hydrometer reading if the main ingredients contain sugar – adjust the weight of sugar still to be added, using the alcoholic strength chart.

5   Stir in the ammonium phosphate, vitamin B_1 tablet, and the yeast. If a yeast starter is being used, this should have been prepared forty-eight hours previously. Cover with a square of linen.

6   Leave for four days, keeping a steady temperature of 21°C (70°F) for white wines, and 24°C (75°F) for rich red wines. An immersion heater as used in the thermostatic control of beer wort temperature will do the trick. These are maximum temperatures, and a steady living-room temperature will serve to keep the yeast active in its work. Stir thrice daily.

7   Strain the liquid through muslin, nylon or plastic mesh into another bucket, then syphon it into a fermentation jar and fit the cork and airlock. Keep at 18°C (64°F), or room heat.

8   After three days (or specific gravity 1.010), funnel in one pint of sugar solution previously prepared and left to cool to 18°C; using half the remaining sugar plus any extra weight of sugar as was ascertained by the use of the hydrometer. For sap wines, dissolve the sugar in one pint of sap, simmered and cooled.

9   Repeat Stage 8, topping up with boiled and cooled water if necessary, using the last of the sugar, and using sap instead of water in the case of sap wines.

10   Rack after seven days, discharging the syphon tube into a funnel in a sterile fermentation jar, so that a cascade occurs. This is the opposite procedure to that required for wines other than dessert. Top up with cool boiled water, or cool boiled sap in the case of sap wines.

11   Repeat Stage 10, but after fourteen days.

12   Rack after a month, topping up as before.

13   Rack after a further month, topping up
again.

14   Rack again after a month if fermentation
has not ceased previously. The fermentation
lock can now be replaced by a small square
of polythene wrapping material secured by a
rubber band, or preferably by the patent
stopper described above. Rack again if a
deposit of sediment should occur, topping up
as before.

15   Bottle, or syphon into bulk containers, all
as previously described.

2 Flower Wines

How To Harvest Flowers

Some flowers can be bought in packets, dried and ready for use, and many flowers which can be used for winemaking are grown in pleasure gardens, while others are free for the gathering on picnic jaunts into the countryside.

They are best harvested as soon as possible after they are in full bloom, when their maximum scent and flavour will be available. The quality of flowers for winemaking also depends upon the time of day when they are gathered. A dry day in the morning, after the dew has evaporated from the plants, but before the sun has had the chance to volatilize their essential oils, is the best time. Otherwise the late afternoon, before evening's dewfall, should be preferred for harvesting.

It is always advisable to handle flowers gently, since it is obvious that bruising dissipates some of the essential oil; the aroma is required from your wine, and not from your hands at gathering time! They should also be spread out as much as possible for a journey home in a car-boot, and not heaped. A porous bag of butter muslin, nylon mesh, or string for instance, dependent upon the size of the flowers to be contained, is an

alternative mode of carriage which will
mitigate against the generation of heat in
heaped produce.

A word of warning is necessary about flowers
which may have received a spraying of
poisonous insecticide, such as can occur on
the perimeter of fields of growing crops, as
well as in a well-maintained floral garden.

RECIPES

Carnation – Social wine

Ingredients

Carnations	4 pints
Raisins	16 oz
Sugar	$2\frac{1}{4}$ lb
Tannin	$\frac{1}{2}$ tsp
Citric acid	$\frac{1}{8}$ tsp
Malic acid	$\frac{1}{4}$ tsp
Tartaric acid	$\frac{1}{4}$ tsp
Ammonium phosphate	2 tsp
3 mg Vitamin B_1	1 tablet
Yeast, G.P.	1 tablet
Water	1 gallon
Lactose	$\frac{3}{4}$ oz

Method
Put the carnation heads into a sterile plastic
bucket, together with the chopped up raisins
and the sugar, and pour boiling water over
them, stirring to dissolve the sugar. Make up
to the one gallon mark (5 litre) with boiled
water. Add the half pint of tea and the acids,
and stir with a sterile plastic or wooden

Monthly Harvest-Time Chart – Fresh Flowers

	Jan	Feb	March	April	May	June	July	Aug	Sept	Oct	Nov	Dec
Carnation						x	x	x				
Coltsfoot			x	x								
Cowslip				x	x							
Dandelion			x	x	x	x	x	x	x	x		
Elder					x	x						
Golden Rod							x	x	x	x		
Hawthorn					x	x						
Hops							x	x	x			
Lime						x	x					
Marigold						x	x	x	x	x	x	
Pansy							x	x				
Primrose				x	x							
Rose						x	x	x				

Basic Formulations

Aperitif Wines

Flowers	3½ pints
Body*	14 oz
Sugar	2¾ lb
Tannin	¼ tsp
Citric acid	⅛ tsp
Malic acid	¼ tsp
Tartaric acid	¼ tsp
Ammonium phosphate	2 tsp
3mg Vitamin B_1	1 tablet
Yeast	1 tablet
Water	1 gallon
Lactose	¾ oz

Table Wines

Flowers	3 pints
Body*	12 oz
Sugar	2 lb
Tannin	¼ tsp
Citric acid	⅛ tsp
Malic acid	¼ tsp
Tartaric acid	¼ tsp
Ammonium phosphate	2 tsp
3mg Vitamin B_1	1 tablet
Yeast	1 tablet
Water	1 gallon

*Body given as dried fruit weight; vegetable, malt, cereal and fresh fruit can also be used in accordance with the previously given table. Flower wines are all light wines, comparatively speaking, and the lactose is optional – you may well prefer a completely dry wine of this type. The flowers should be shaken down in the measuring jug, but not pressed down. Elderflower and Golden Rod – use ¼ the measure of such strong flavoured/scented flowers.

Sparkling Table Wines	
Flowers	3½ pints
Body*	14 oz
Sugar	2½ lb
Tannin	¼ tsp
Citric acid	⅛ tsp
Malic acid	¼ tsp
Tartaric acid	¼ tsp
Ammonium phosphate	2 tsp
3mg Vitamin B₁	1 tablet
Yeast	1 tablet
Water	1 gallon
Lactose	½ oz

Social Wines	
Flowers	4 pints
Body*	16 oz
Sugar	2¾ lb
Tannin	½ tsp
Citric acid	⅛ tsp
Malic acid	¼ tsp
Tartaric acid	¼ tsp
Ammonium phosphate	2 tsp
3mg Vitamin B¹	1 tablet
Yeast	1 tablet
Water	1 gallon
Lactose	¾ oz

*Body given as dried fruit weight; vegetable, malt, cereal and fresh fruit can also be used in accordance with the previously given table. Flower wines are all light wines, comparatively speaking, and the lactose is optional – you may well prefer a completely dry wine of this type. The flowers should be shaken down in the measuring jug, but not pressed down. Elderflower and Golden Rod – use ¼ the measure of such strong flavoured/scented flowers.

Basic Formulations

Dessert Wines

Flowers	5 pints	Tartaric acid	$\frac{1}{4}$ tsp
Body*	20 oz	Ammonium phosphate	2 tsp
Sugar	$3\frac{1}{4}$ lb	3mg Vitamin B_1	1 tablet
Tannin	$\frac{1}{2}$ tsp	Yeast	1 tablet
Citric acid	$\frac{1}{8}$ tsp	Water	1 gallon
Malic Acid	$\frac{1}{4}$ tsp	Lactose	$1\frac{1}{2}$ oz

*Body given as dried fruit weight; vegetable, malt, cereal and fresh fruit can also be used in accordance with the previously given table. Flower wines are all light wines, comparatively speaking, and the lactose is optional – you may well prefer a completely dry wine of this type. The flowers should be shaken down in the measuring jug, but not pressed down. Elderflower and Golden Rod – use $\frac{1}{4}$ the measure of such strong flavoured/scented flowers.

spoon to dissolve them. Cover with a sheet of
linen and leave to cool to 21°C (70°F). Now
take a hydrometer reading, and adjust the
sugar content, if necessary, according to the
previously given Alcoholic Strength Chart.
Stir in the ammonium phosphate, the vitamin
tablet, and the crushed yeast. If a yeast starter
is being used, this should have been
prepared forty-eight hours previously. Leave
covered for seven days at a steady
temperature of 21°C (70°F), or at room
temperature, and stir vigorously thrice daily.
Strain through nylon mesh into another
sterile plastic bucket, allow to settle, and then
syphon into a fermentation jar. Top up to the
neck with boiled and cooled water, if required,
fit the cork and fermentation lock, and keep at
18°C (64°F), or at room temperature for one
month. Rack and top up as before. Rack and
top up after a further month. Repeat after
another month, and fit a patent ball-bearing
stopper. Repeat in the event of any further
sedimentation. Syphon into bottles or other
storage containers, adding the lactose
dissolved in a little of the wine, after a total
winemaking time of six months, and store at a
temperature of about 7–10°C (45–50°F).

Coltsfoot – Social wine

The yellow flower appears on a solitary thick
stem, well in advance of the large, thick,
heart-shaped leaves, and is to be found on
roadside and other open wasteland very early
in the year.

Ingredients

Coltsfoot flowers	4 pints
Sultanas	16 oz
Sugar	$2\frac{1}{4}$ lb
Tannin	$\frac{1}{2}$ tsp
Citric acid	$\frac{1}{8}$ tsp
Malic acid	$\frac{1}{4}$ tsp
Tartaric acid	$\frac{1}{4}$ tsp
Ammonium phosphate	2 tsp
3 mg Vitamin B_1	1 tablet
Yeast, Sauterne	1 tablet
Water	1 gallon
Lactose	$\frac{3}{4}$ oz

Method

This is the same as for Carnation social wine; the whole heads of the flowers are used.

Cowslip – Dessert wine

Only the actual flowers should be used in this wine, and all the greenery must be discarded; you'll need to gather quite a few bunches of them for separation at home.

Ingredients

Cowslips	5 pints
Sultanas	20 oz
Sugar	$2\frac{1}{2}$ lb
Tannin	$\frac{1}{2}$ tsp
Citric acid	$\frac{1}{8}$ tsp
Malic acid	$\frac{1}{4}$ tsp
Tartaric acid	$\frac{1}{4}$ tsp
Ammonium phosphate	2 tsp
3 mg Vitamin B_1	1 tablet

Yeast, Sauterne	1 tablet
Water	1 gallon
Lactose	1½ oz

Method

Pour three pints of tapwater into a sterile
plastic bucket containing the cowslips and
the chopped up sultanas, stir in a crushed
Campden tablet, and leave covered with a
sheet of linen for twenty-four hours. Then
dissolve half of the total weight of sugar to
be used in a pint of boiling water, and add to
the contents of the bucket. Add the half a
pint of tannin and the acids, and stir with a
spoon to dissolve the chemicals. Make up to
the six pint mark only, with boiled water.
Allow to cool to 21°C (70°F), keeping covered
with a sheet of linen. Take a hydrometer
reading, and adjust the weight of sugar still
to be added, using the Alcoholic Strength
Chart. Stir in the ammonium phosphate, the
vitamin tablet and the yeast. Cover with a
square of linen sheeting, and leave for four
days at a temperature of 21°C (70°F), or at
room temperature, stirring thrice daily. Strain
through nylon mesh into another sterile
bucket, allow to settle, then syphon into a
fermentation jar, fitting the cork and airlock.
Keep at 18°C (64°F), or at room heat for three
days, to specific gravity 1.010. Funnel in one pint
of sugar solution which has cooled to 18°C,
using half the remaining sugar, plus any
extra weight of sugar which was indicated
when the hydrometer reading was taken.
After a further three days, funnel in the

remaining sugar, dissolved in one pint of
boiling water and cooled to 18°C. Top up with
boiled and cooled water if this is required.
Rack after seven days, cascading into the
sterile fermentation jar, and topping up again
to the bottom of the neck of the fermentation
jar. Rack again after fourteen days. Rack again
after a month, topping up as before. Rack
once more after a further month. If
fermentation is still proceeding in another
month's time, rack and top up again. A patent
ball-bearing stopper can now replace the
fermentation lock. If a sedimentary deposit
occurs, rack again. After a total winemaking
time of six months, syphon into bottles or
bulk storage containers, and store at a
temperature of about 7–10°C (45–50°F). The
lactose can be added at bottling time, or
when pouring into a decanter.

Dandelion – Table wine

The whole heads of this flower are used, but
be careful not to include any stalk. You may
prefer this wine sweet, in which case add
lactose to taste.

Ingredients

Dandelions	3 pints
Sultanas	12 oz
Sugar	$1\frac{3}{4}$ lb
Tannin	$\frac{1}{4}$ tsp
Citric acid	$\frac{1}{8}$ tsp
Malic acid	$\frac{1}{4}$ tsp
Tartaric acid	$\frac{1}{4}$ tsp

Ammonium phosphate	2 tsp
3mg Vitamin B$_1$	1 tablet
Yeast, Graves	1 tablet
Water	1 gallon

Method

Pour boiling water into a sterile plastic bucket containing the dandelions, chopped up sultanas, and the sugar, stirring to dissolve the sugar. Make up to the one gallon mark with boiled water. Stir in the acids and the quarter-pint of tea. Cover with linen sheeting, and leave to cool to 21°C (70°F). Take a hydrometer reading, and adjust the sugar requirement, if necessary, in accordance with the Alcoholic Strength Chart. Stir in the ammonium phosphate, the vitamin tablet and the yeast. Leave covered with a square of linen for three days at a steady temperature of 21°C, or at room temperature, stirring thrice daily. Strain through nylon mesh into another sterile bucket, allow to settle, and then syphon into a fermentation jar, top up to the neck with boiled and cooled water, if required, and fit the cork and fermentation lock. Keep at 18°C (64°F), or at room temperature for a month. Rack, and top up as before. After another month, rack and top up again. Repeat the racking and topping up after a further month, and replace the fermentation lock by a patent ball-bearing stopper. If any further sedimentation occurs, rack again. After a total wine-making time of six months, syphon into bulk containers or bottles, and store at 7–10°C (45–50°F).

Elder – Sparkling table wine

Cut the elderflowers from their stalks with
the aid of a pair of scissors.

Ingredients

Elderflowers	1 pint
Rhubarb	20 oz
Sugar	$2\frac{1}{2}$ lb
Tannin	$\frac{1}{4}$ tsp
Citric acid	$\frac{1}{8}$ tsp
Malic acid	$\frac{1}{4}$ tsp
Tartaric acid	$\frac{1}{4}$ tsp
Ammonium phosphate	2 tsp
3 mg Vitamin B_1	1 tablet
Yeast, Champagne	1 tablet
Water	1 gallon
Lactose	$\frac{1}{2}$ oz

Method

Wash the rhubarb in cold water, cut it into
one inch lengths, and squash it up in a sterile
plastic bucket with the aid of a stainless steel
potato masher. Pour in sufficient previously
boiled cool water to cover it, stir in $\frac{1}{4}$ oz of
precipitated chalk, and leave to effervesce for
twenty-four hours, covered with a sheet of
linen. This will neutralize the unwanted oxalic
acid in the rhubarb. Bring it to the boil in a
boiler, and pour it over the elderflowers and
sugar now contained in the sterile plastic
bucket. Stir to dissolve the sugar, using a
sterile spoon. Make up to the one gallon
mark with boiled water, and add the acids
together with the quarter of a pint of tea,

stirring to dissolve the chemicals. Cover with
linen sheeting and leave to cool to 21°C
(70°F). Stir in the ammonium phosphate,
vitamin tablet, and the yeast. Leave covered
for five days, keeping a steady temperature of
21°C, or at room temperature, and stirring
thrice daily. Strain through nylon mesh into
another bucket, allow to settle, and syphon
into a fermentation jar, topping up to the neck
with boiled and cooled water. Fit the cork and
fermentation lock, and keep at 18°C (64°F), or
room temperature. Rack after a month, topping
up as before, and save some of the yeast
deposit in a small sterile bottle in the
refrigerator. Rack after a further month, not
neglecting to top up as before. After another
month, rack again, topping up as before and
refitting the fermentation lock, or replacing
it by a patent ball-bearing stopper. In the
event of further sedimentation, rack again.
Bottle in champagne bottles after a total
wine-making time of six months – a yeast
starter must be prepared, at the least, three
days before bottling, using the yeast from the
refrigerator. A teaspoonful of this and of
sugar, together with a proportion of lactose,
will be added to each bottle before wiring
down. Store at 7–10°C (45–50°F).

Golden Rod – Dessert wine

These flowers contain tannin.

Ingredients

Golden Rod	1$\frac{1}{4}$ pints
Raisins	20 oz

Sugar	$2\frac{1}{2}$ lb
Citric acid	$\frac{1}{8}$ tsp
Malic acid	$\frac{1}{4}$ tsp
Tartaric acid	$\frac{1}{4}$ tsp
Ammonium phosphate	2 tsp
3 mg Vitamin B_1	1 tablet
Yeast, Sherry	1 tablet
Water	1 gallon
Lactose	$1\frac{1}{2}$ oz

Method
This is the same as for Cowslip dessert
wine, but the hot water method can be used.
Pour four pints of boiling water into a sterile
plastic bucket containing the flowers, half of
the total weight of sugar to be used, and the
chopped up raisins, stirring to dissolve the
sugar; thereafter proceeding as has been
described.

Hawthorn – Aperitif wine

Ingredients

Hawthorn blossom	$3\frac{1}{2}$ pints
Wheat	8 oz
Raisins	6 oz
Sugar	$2\frac{3}{4}$ lb
Tannin	$\frac{1}{4}$ tsp
Citric acid	$\frac{1}{8}$ tsp
Malic acid	$\frac{1}{4}$ tsp
Tartaric acid	$\frac{1}{4}$ tsp
Ammonium phosphate	2 tsp
3mg Vitamin B_1	1 tablet
Yeast, Madeira	1 tablet
Water	1 gallon
Lactose	$\frac{3}{4}$ oz

Method

Pour tapwater into a sterile plastic bucket containing the hawthorn blossom, the cracked (opened up by the use of a sterile rolling pin, but not crushed) wheat, and the chopped up raisins, stir in three crushed Campden tablets, and leave covered with a linen sheet for twenty-four hours. Dissolve the sugar in boiling water, and add to the contents of the bucket. Make up to the one gallon mark with boiled water. Stir in the acids and add the quarter of a pint of tea. Leave to cool to 21°C (70°F), keeping covered with a square of linen sheeting. Stir in the ammonium phosphate, vitamin tablet, and the yeast. If a yeast starter is being used, this should have been prepared forty-eight hours previously. Cover with linen sheeting, and leave for seven days, keeping a steady temperature of 21°C (70°F), or at room temperature. Stir thrice daily. Strain through nylon mesh into another bucket, and allow to settle. Syphon into a fermentation jar, top up to the neck with boiled and cooled water, if required, fit the cork and the fermentation lock, and keep at 18°C (64°F), or at room temperature. Rack after a month, and top up. Rack again after a further month. Rack again after another month, and replace the fermentation lock by a patent ball-bearing release valve stopper. After a total winemaking time of six months, syphon into bottles or bulk container, and store at 7–10°C (45–50°F). Add the lactose, in a solution of a little of the wine, when pouring into the decanter.

Hops – Social wine

Ingredients

Hops	1 oz
Root Ginger	1 oz
Raisins	1 lb
Sugar	$2\frac{1}{4}$ lb
Tannin	$\frac{1}{2}$ tsp
Citric acid	$\frac{1}{8}$ tsp
Malic acid	$\frac{1}{4}$ tsp
Tartaric acid	$\frac{1}{4}$ tsp
Ammonium phosphate	2 tsp
3mg Vitamin B_1	1 tablet
Yeast, G.P.	1 tablet
Water	1 gallon
Lactose	$\frac{3}{4}$ oz

Method

This is the same as for Carnation social wine, except that the root ginger is boiled in the water for half an hour, and then for a further half an hour with the hops added; the strained liquor is then poured into a sterile plastic bucket containing the chopped up raisins and the sugar, stirring to dissolve the sugar. Make up to the one gallon (5 litre) mark with boiled water, and then proceed as described.

Lime – Dessert wine

The long bracts are collected with the flowers, which should be just nicely opened. The flowers break off easily, and require careful handling.

Ingredients

Lime Flowers	5 pints
Barley	8 oz
Raisins	12 oz
Sugar	3 lb
Tannin	$\frac{1}{2}$ tsp
Citric acid	$\frac{1}{8}$ tsp
Malic acid	$\frac{1}{4}$ tsp
Tartaric acid	$\frac{1}{4}$ tsp
Ammonium phosphate	2 tsp
3mg Vitamin B_1	1 tablet
Yeast, G.P.	1 tablet
Water	1 gallon
Lactose	$1\frac{1}{2}$ oz

Method

This is the same as for Cowslip dessert wine, but the barley should be cracked just open before being used with the raisins.

Marigold – Dessert wine

The marsh marigold should not be countenanced; the flower used is the Calendula or common garden marigold, and it will provide petals right through to November if the flower heads are removed as they become ready.

Ingredients

Marigold petals	5 pints
Sultanas	20 oz
Sugar	$2\frac{1}{2}$ lb
Tannin	$\frac{1}{2}$ tsp
Citric acid	$\frac{1}{8}$ tsp

Malic acid	$\frac{1}{4}$ tsp
Tartaric acid	$\frac{1}{4}$ tsp
Ammonium phosphate	2 tsp
3mg Vitamin B_1	1 tablet
Yeast, Sauterne	1 tablet
Water	1 gallon
Lactose	$1\frac{1}{2}$ oz

Method
This is the same as for Cowslip dessert wine.

Pansy – Dessert wine

Ingredients

Pansy	5 pints
Bananas	24 oz
Raisins	8 oz
Sugar	3 lb
Tannin	$\frac{1}{2}$ tsp
Citric acid	$\frac{1}{8}$ tsp
Malic acid	$\frac{1}{4}$ tsp
Tartaric acid	$\frac{1}{4}$ tsp
Ammonium phosphate	2 tsp
3mg Vitamin B_1	1 tablet
Yeast, G.P.	1 tablet
Water	1 gallon
Lactose	$1\frac{1}{2}$ oz

Method
Pour three pints of boiling water into a sterile
plastic bucket containing the mashed up
bananas and the chopped up (or minced)
raisins; leave covered to cool, and then add
the pansy heads, a crushed Campden tablet,
and half a teaspoonful of Pectinol (to

neutralize the pectin in the bananas). Leave covered with a sheet of linen for twenty-four hours. Thereafter, proceed as for Cowslip dessert wine.

Primrose – Table wine

Make sure that none of the green stalk is included in your primrose must, or the wine may have a bitter taste.

Ingredients

Primroses	3 pints
Sultanas	12 oz
Sugar	1¾ lb
Tannin	¼ tsp
Citric acid	⅛ tsp
Malic acid	¼ tsp
Tartaric acid	¼ tsp
Ammonium phosphate	2 tsp
3mg Vitamin B_1	1 tablet
Yeast, Hock	1 tablet
Water	1 gallon

Method

This is the same as for Dandelion table wine except that the cold water method of extraction is used. Pour tapwater into a plastic bucket containing the primroses and the chopped or minced sultanas, stir in three crushed Campden tablets, and leave covered with a sheet of linen for twenty-four hours. Dissolve the sugar in boiling water, and add to the contents of the bucket. Make up to the one gallon mark with previously boiled water, and then proceed as for the Dandelion wine.

Rose – Social wine

Use dark red, strongly scented rose petals. If
they are not from your own garden, you will
normally have no difficulty in obtaining
permission to remove the petals of fully
blown roses from their heads on the bush,
but make sure that they have not been
sprayed with poisonous insecticide after the
most recent rainfall.

Ingredients

Rosepetals	4 pints
Raisins	1 lb
Sugar	$2\frac{1}{4}$ lb
Tannin	$\frac{1}{2}$ tsp
Citric acid	$\frac{1}{8}$ tsp
Malic acid	$\frac{1}{4}$ tsp
Tartaric acid	$\frac{1}{4}$ tsp
Ammonium phosphate	2 tsp
3mg Vitamin B_1	1 tablet
Yeast, Burgundy	1 tablet
Water	1 gallon
Lactose	$\frac{3}{4}$ oz

Method
This is the same as for Carnation social wine.

3 Leaf Wines

How To Harvest Leaves

Leaves are best gathered just before the tree
or bush is due to flower, and on a dry day
when the leaves are free from morning or
evening dew.

As in the case of flowers, leaves should be
spread out as much as possible for a journey
home in the car-boot, and they should not be
heaped. A nylon mesh or string bag, which
can be hung up in the car on coat hangers, is
an alternative means of carriage which will
mitigate against the unwanted generation of
heat in heaped leaves.

Once again a warning is called for against the
gathering of leaves which could have been
contaminated by the spraying of insecticide.
The leaves should invariably be washed in
cold running water to remove dust and the
like.

RECIPES

Bramble – Table wine
Use double the amount of young bramble tips
given in the basic formulation for leaf wines,

Monthly Harvest-Time Chart – Leaves

	Jan	Feb	March	April	May	June	July	Aug	Sept	Oct	Nov	Dec
Bramble					x	x	x					
Lavender							x	x	x			
Oak							x	x				
Pelargonium				x	x							
Tea					x	x	x	x				
Vine			Will be used in dried form from the packet									
Walnut				Pruning time	x							
Red Dock						x	x	x				

Basic Formulations

Aperitif Wines

Leaves	4 pints
Body*	14 oz
Sugar	$2\frac{3}{4}$ lb
Citric acid	$\frac{1}{8}$ tsp
Malic acid	$\frac{1}{4}$ tsp
Tartaric acid	$\frac{1}{4}$ tsp
Ammonium phosphate	2 tsp
3mg Vitamin B_1	1 tablet
Yeast	1 tablet
Water	1 gallon
Lactose	$1\frac{1}{2}$ oz

Table Wines

Leaves	3 pints
Body*	12 oz
Sugar	2 lb
Citric acid	$\frac{1}{8}$ tsp
Malic acid	$\frac{1}{4}$ tsp
Tartaric acid	$\frac{1}{4}$ tsp
Ammonium phosphate	2 tsp
3mg Vitamin B_1	1 tablet
Yeast	1 tablet
Water	1 gallon

*Body given as dried fruit weight; vegetable, malt, cereal, and fresh fruit can also be used in accordance with the table given previously. The amount of leaves to use will also vary according to their strength of flavour – walnut leaves have a strong flavour. Tannin is present in most leaves, but will be added when absent.

Basic Formulations

Sparkling Table Wines

	4 pints
Leaves	
Body*	14 oz
Sugar	2½ lb
Citric acid	⅛ tsp
Malic acid	¼ tsp
Tartaric acid	¼ tsp
Ammonium phosphate	2 tsp
3mg Vitamin B$_1$	1 tablet
Yeast	1 tablet
Water	1 gallon
Lactose	1 oz

Social Wines

	5 pints
Leaves	
Body*	16 oz
Sugar	2¾ lb
Citric acid	¼ tsp
Malic acid	½ tsp
Tartaric acid	½ tsp
Ammonium phosphate	2 tsp
3mg Vitamin B$_1$	1 tablet
Yeast	1 tablet
Water	1 gallon
Lactose	1½ oz

*Body given as dried fruit weight; vegetable, malt, cereal, and fresh fruit can also be used in accordance with the table given previously. The amount of leaves to use will also vary according to their strength of flavour – walnut leaves have a strong flavour. Tannin is present in most leaves, but will be added when absent.

Dessert Wines

Leaves	7 pints	Ammonium phosphate	2 tsp
Body*	20 oz	3mg Vitamin B$_1$	1 tablet
Sugar	3¼ lb	Yeast	1 tablet
Citric acid	¼ tsp	Water	1 gallon
Malic acid	½ tsp	Lactose	3 oz
Tartaric acid	½ tsp		

*Body given as dried fruit weight; vegetable, malt, cereal, and fresh fruit can also be used in accordance with the table given previously. The amount of leaves to use will also vary according to their strength of flavour – walnut leaves have a strong flavour. Tannin is present in most leaves, but will be added when absent.

since their flavour is much more delicate
than average.

Ingredients

Bramble tips	6 pints
Sultanas	$\frac{3}{4}$ lb
Sugar	$1\frac{3}{4}$ lb
Citric acid	$\frac{1}{8}$ tsp
Malic acid	$\frac{1}{4}$ tsp
Tartaric acid	$\frac{1}{4}$ tsp
Ammonium phosphate	2 tsp
3mg Vitamin B$_1$	1 tablet
Yeast, Bordeaux	1 tablet
Water	1 gallon

Method

Boil the tender young washed bramble tips in
water for three quarters of an hour, and then
strain into a sterile plastic bucket containing
the chopped up sultanas and the sugar,
stirring to dissolve the sugar. Make up to the
one gallon (5 litre) mark with boiled water, stir
in the acids, allow to cool to 21°C (70°F) while
covered with a square of linen sheeting. Take
a hydrometer reading, and adjust the sugar
content as necessary, with the aid of the
Alcoholic Strength Chart. Stir in the ammonium
phosphate, the vitamin tablet, and the yeast
or yeast starter. Cover with the linen sheet
and leave for three days at 21°C (70°F), or at
room temperature, stirring twice daily. Strain
through nylon mesh into another sterile
bucket, allow to settle, and syphon into a
fermentation jar. Top up to the neck with
boiled and cooled water, if required, and fit the

cork and fermentation lock. Keep at 18°C
(64°F), or at room temperature for a month,
and then rack and top up again. Rack and top
up after another month, and repeat after a
further month; again after another month.
Bottle, or syphon into bulk container after a
total winemaking time of six months, and store
at 7–10°C (45–50°F).

Lavender – Social wine

Lavender has an exceptionally strong flavour
and bouquet, so we will halve the amount
given in the basic formulation for leaf wines.
Remove the leaves from the stalks, and discard
the stalks.

Ingredients

Lavender	2½ pints
Raisins	1 lb
Sugar	2¼ lb
Tannin	½ tsp
Citric acid	¼ tsp
Malic acid	½ tsp
Tartaric acid	½ tsp
Ammonium phosphate	2 tsp
3mg Vitamin B$_1$	1 tablet
Yeast, G.P.	1 tablet
Water	1 gallon
Lactose	1½ oz

Method

Pour boiling water into a sterile plastic bucket
containing the washed lavender leaves,
chopped up raisins, and the sugar, stirring to

dissolve the sugar. Make up to the one gallon (5 litre) mark with boiled water. Stir in the acids, and the half pint of tea, cover with a square of linen sheeting, and leave to cool to 21°C (70°F). Take a hydrometer reading, and adjust the sugar content, as necessary, in accordance with the Alcoholic Strength Chart for social wines. Stir in the ammonium phosphate, the vitamin tablet, and the yeast or yeast starter. Cover with a square of linen sheeting, and keep at 21°C (70°F), or at room temperature for seven days, stirring thrice daily. Strain through nylon mesh into another sterile plastic bucket, allow to settle, syphon into a fermentation jar, and top up if necessary with boiled and cooled water. Fit the cork and fermentation lock, and keep at 18°C (64°F) for a month. Rack and top up, repeating after a further month, and after one more month. Bottle, or syphon into a bulk container after a total winemaking time of six months, and store at 7–10°C (45–50°F). Add the lactose when transferring the wine into a decanter.

Oak – Dessert wine

Ingredients

Oakleaves	7 pints
Raisins	20 oz
Sugar	2¾ lb
Citric acid	¼ tsp
Malic acid	½ tsp
Tartaric acid	½ tsp
Ammonium phosphate	2 tsp

3mg Vitamin B$_1$	1 tablet
Yeast, Sherry	1 tablet
Water	1 gallon
Lactose	3 oz

Method

Pour four pints of boiling water into a sterile
plastic bucket containing the rinsed oakleaves,
the chopped up raisins, and half the total
weight of sugar to be used, stirring to dissolve
the sugar. Stir in the acids, and make up to
the six pint mark only, with boiled water. Allow
to cool to 21°C (70°F), keeping covered with
linen sheeting. Take a hydrometer reading,
and adjust the sugar content according to the
previously given Alcoholic Strength Chart. Stir
in the ammonium phosphate, the vitamin
tablet, and the yeast; if a yeast starter is being
used, it should have been prepared forty-eight
hours previously. Cover with a square of
linen and leave for four days at 21°C (70°F),
or at room temperature, stirring thrice daily.
Strain through nylon mesh into another
bucket, then syphon into a fermentation jar,
fitting the cork and the fermentation lock.
Keep at 18°C, or at room heat for three days
(or specific gravity 1.010). Funnel in one pint of
sugar solution previously left to cool from
boiling point to 18°C; using half the
remaining sugar requirement as was indicated
by the previous hydrometer reading. After a
further three days, add the remaining sugar in
solution, topping up to the neck of the
fermentation jar with boiled and cooled water,
if required. Rack after seven days, using the

previously described cascade method, and
top up as before. Rack again after fourteen
days. Thereafter, rack at monthly intervals
until no more sediment is deposited. Bottle,
or syphon into a bulk container. The lactose is
added, to taste, at decanting time.

Pelargonium (Quercifolium) – Social wine

This is a type of geranium.

Ingredients

Pelargonium leaves	5 pints
Sultanas	1 lb
Sugar	$2\frac{1}{4}$ lb
Tannin	$\frac{1}{2}$ tsp
Citric acid	$\frac{1}{4}$ tsp
Malic acid	$\frac{1}{2}$ tsp
Tartaric acid	$\frac{1}{2}$ tsp
Ammonium phosphate	2 tsp
3mg Vitamin B_1	1 tablet
Yeast, G.P.	1 tablet
Water	1 gallon
Lactose	$1\frac{1}{2}$ oz

Method
This is the same as for Lavender social wine.

Tea – Social wine

This is the dried leaf, of course, and tea
bags are a very convenient form to use since
they are self-filtering. They also provide a
means of securing an exact measure of the
leaf and subsequent recipes can thus be easily
adjusted to suit individual taste.

Ingredients

Teabags	8
Raisins	1 lb
Sugar	2¼ lb
Citric acid	¼ tsp
Malic acid	½ tsp
Tartaric acid	½ tsp
Ammonium phosphate	2 tsp
3mg Vitamin B$_1$	1 tablet
Yeast, Sherry	1 tablet
Water	1 gallon
Lactose	1½ oz

Method

This is the same as for Lavender social wine, but no additional tannin is required, of course, and there is no dust or other impurities to wash away from the tea leaves.

Vine – Table wine

Make sure that the vines have not been sprayed prior to pruning, and in any case give the leaves, tendrils, and young shoots a good rinsing in cold running water before using them for winemaking, after which, cut them up into small pieces about an inch long. Cut only the green parts, of course, and not the ripe wood.

Ingredients

Vine prunings	3 pints
Sultanas	¾ lb
Sugar	1¾ lb
Citric acid	⅛ tsp

Malic acid	$\frac{1}{4}$ tsp
Tartaric acid	$\frac{1}{4}$ tsp
Ammonium phosphate	2 tsp
3mg Vitamin B_1	1 tablet
Yeast, Hock	1 tablet
Water	1 gallon

Method
Pour boiling water into a sterile plastic bucket
containing the vine prunings, the chopped up
sultanas, and the sugar, stirring to dissolve
the sugar. Make up to the one gallon (5 litre)
mark with boiled water, and then proceed as
for Bramble table wine.

Walnut – Dessert wine

The walnut tree is described in the following
chapter, and that description will enable
you to recognize it for the purpose of
leaf-gathering. The leaves have a very
pronounced flavour, and for that reason use
only a fraction of the amount of leaves given
in the basic formulation for dessert wines.
Tannin is a natural constituent of the leaves,
and none need be added.

Ingredients

Walnut leaves	1 pint
Sultanas	20 oz
Sugar	$2\frac{1}{2}$ lb
Citric acid	$\frac{1}{4}$ tsp
Malic acid	$\frac{1}{2}$ tsp
Tartaric acid	$\frac{1}{2}$ tsp
Ammonium phosphate	2 tsp

3 mg Vitamin B$_1$	1 tablet
Yeast, Sauterne	1 tablet
Water	1 gallon
Lactose	3 oz

Method
This is the same as that used for Oakleaf
dessert wine.

Red Dock – Social wine

Ingredients

Red Dock	5 pints
Currants	1 lb
Sugar	2$\frac{1}{4}$ lb
Tannin	$\frac{1}{2}$ tsp
Citric acid	$\frac{1}{4}$ tsp
Malic acid	$\frac{1}{2}$ tsp
Tartaric acid	$\frac{1}{2}$ tsp
Ammonium phosphate	2 tsp
3mg Vitamin B$_1$	1 tablet
Yeast, G.P.	1 tablet
Water	1 gallon
Lactose	1$\frac{1}{2}$ oz

Method
This is the same as for Lavender social wine.

4 Sap Wines

The Trees Described

The trees which are regularly tapped for the purpose of winemaking are the Birch, Sycamore and Walnut. You may gain the opportunity to sample the sap of the Date, Coconut and Oil Palm trees, and of the Sugar Maple, but the Birch, Sycamore and Walnut will remain the more readily available to the vast majority of winemakers.

It will be helpful to know where to look for these three trees and how to identify them.

The Silver Birch is more common in the east and south of England, especially in woods and on heaths in light but not chalky soil. The White Birch is frequently to be found in western and northern Britain, once again in woods and on heaths, but in damp, peaty soil. The Dwarf Birch is fairly common in bogs, and on the moors in Scotland. Where there is the easily recognizable heather and pine tree, the Birch tree will usually be found too.

The Silver Birch is a graceful, light and dainty looking deciduous tree with a slender trunk, from 40 to 70 feet tall when fully grown. It terminates with a crown of long, drooping, secondary branches. The lower bark on mature trees (which are the ones we seek) is craggy, deeply grooved, and almost black in colour, while the upper bark is thin, smooth, peeling, silvery-white in colour, with black markings, and often revealing a pink coloured bark where the outer bark has come away. The long stalked, shiny, dark green, leaves, nearly two inches long are a broad oval, almost triangular shape with long points, and their perimeter is doubly serrated. The reddish-brown or yellowish male hanging catkins are narrow, and about two inches long, growing near the ends of the twigs. The female catkins are shorter and broader than their male counterparts, greenish in colour, and about one and a quarter inches long. The two-winged fruit is very small.

The White Birch is similar to the Silver Birch, except that the secondary branches are spreading and erect, the whole of the bark is smooth and a dull silvery-grey in colour, the scales on the twigs are replaced by hairs, the long points are not in evidence on the lozenge-shaped leaves, which are a dull green in colour and their margins have irregular serrations. It is usually slightly smaller than the Silver Birch, growing to a mature height of 60 feet.

The Dwarf Birch sometimes appears as a tree up to 20 feet tall, but usually it is found as a shrub growing up to 8 feet in height, with stiff spreading branches which often grow along the ground. The leaves are a glossy

bright green in colour, much toothed, nearly
disc-shaped, almost stalkless, about half an
inch long, with a bluntly toothed margin. The
catkins are stalkless, the male are
cylindrical-shaped, spreading, and three
quarters of an inch long, whilst the female are
borne almost erect, and are half an inch long.

The wood of the Birch tree will be found to be
white and hard when drilled for tapping.

The sweet, sugary sap is abundant when
rising, and may be seen exuding in a steady
drip from any newly damaged limb of the tree
in the early spring.

Birch tree sap is obtained for winemaking
purposes by tapping the tree in the first
fortnight of the month of March; a sweet
candy can be made by the simple
evaporation of the sap.

The Sycamore tree is to be found throughout
this country, and is well known as a park
tree. It can serve a valuable service as a strong
windbreak, and has often been planted near
the sea coast, and on upland farms for this
purpose. It grows to a height of 40 to 60 feet.

It is commonly but wrongly known in Scotland
as the 'Plane' tree, to which family it owes no
allegiance, being a member of the Maple
family. The true Plane tree has its leaves and
buds sited alternately along the branches,

whereas the Sycamore has them placed in pairs opposite to each other.

The bark is smooth and grey in colour, but on the trunks of old trees it is rough and yellowish-brown in colour and is often found to be flaking off in rectangular pieces. The wood is a very pale brown or creamy-white in colour, and the sap which emerges when the tree is tapped is not milky.

The leaves are borne on long reddish coloured stalks, have five pointed lobes, and are generally similar to the maple-leaf emblem on the Canadian flag. The margins of the leaves have rounded indentations.

You can pinpoint a Sycamore tree, for your information and action in the spring, by means of its flowers and fruit. The flowers appear from April to June, and hang from the tree in long clusters which are greenish-yellow in colour, and have a faint characteristic scent.

The two-seeded fruit has a broad curved wing on either side, the whole of roughly boomerang shape, and it spins to the ground when detached from the branch of the tree from which it has been hanging; it is green in colour at first, turning brown by the time the month of October arrives.

The Walnut tree is cultivated as an orchard tree in Britain, and is also to be found in hedgerows and on waste ground, where it is readily self-sown. It is a deciduous tree, growing to a height of up to 100 feet, and has wide-spreading branches with an upward trend.

The bark of the tree trunk is pale ash-grey in colour, and smooth in texture on young trees, fissured on older ones.

The compound leaves comprise five to eleven leaflets, which are elliptic in shape, three to six inches long, appear alternately on each side of the mid-rib, and increase in size to the largest terminal leaflet. When a leaf is crushed between the fingers a rich, fruity aroma is obtained, making the tree easily recognizable.

The sapwood which will be removed when the tree is bored for sap is a pale greyish-brown in colour.

The flowers will also be a means of recognition, which will enable you to mark it down for sap-tapping in the following March. The male flowers are long, curved, slender, pendulant catkins, whilst the female flowers appear in solitary isolation, or two or three together. At the early stage of fruiting, the then soft-shelled nut is hidden in a soft green covering. The mature nut-casings are, of course, familiar to everyone.

Now that you have some idea where to find these trees, and how to recognize them, we can discuss the sap-tapping procedure.

How To Tap Trees For Sap

In the first fortnight of March, before the
leaf-buds open up, take a brace and bit, the
latter of quarter of an inch diameter, and bore
a one inch deep hole, just through the bark,
slanting upwards, and at about eighteen
inches from the ground, into the trunk of a
mature tree. Please note that young trees can
be killed by this tapping of their rising sap,
and they should never be used for this
purpose – in any case their yield of sap would
not be adequate for our purpose; suitable
tree trunks are about nine inches in
diameter. Do not bore deeper than one inch,
or you may be penetrating into the older wood
and beyond the path of the rising sap. Insert
the end of a 2 ft long × $\frac{1}{4}$ inch diameter
piece of plastic tube into the hole, and fix it
in place with sellotape. Pass the other end
into a fermentation jar stood firmly on the
ground nearby, and plug the neck with a short
length of cotton wool. In normal circumstances,
the jar should fill up within two to three days.
Before you take away your equipment, neatly
plug the hole in the tree with a short length of
quarter of an inch wood dowelling. You may
wish to remove each daily collection of sap,
in which case it can be kept sterile at home
with the use of Campden tablets in the
proportion of one for every three pints of sap;
and kept corked in the bottle, of course. Do
not take more than one gallon of sap from
any one tree in any given year, or the tree will
suffer.

Basic Formulations

Aperitif Wines

	1 gallon
Sap	14 oz
Body*	
Sugar (to S.G. 1.105)	
Tannin	$\frac{1}{2}$ tsp
Citric acid	$\frac{1}{4}$ tsp
Malic acid	$\frac{1}{2}$ tsp
Tartaric acid	$\frac{1}{2}$ tsp
Ammonium phosphate	1 tsp
3mg Vitamin B$_1$	1 tablet
Yeast	1 tablet
Lactose	2 oz

Table Wines

	1 gallon
Sap	14 oz
Body*	
Sugar (to S.G. 1.075)	
Tannin	$\frac{1}{2}$ tsp
Citric acid	$\frac{1}{8}$ tsp
Malic acid	$\frac{1}{4}$ tsp
Tartaric acid	$\frac{1}{4}$ tsp
Ammonium phosphate	1 tsp
3mg Vitamin B$_1$	1 tablet
Yeast	1 tablet

*Body given as dried fruit weight; this will be one of the grape derivatives (sultanas, raisins, currants), dates or figs. Vegetable, malt, cereal and fresh fruit can also be used in accordance with the previously given table.

Basic Formulations

Sparkling Table Wines	1 gallon
Sap	
Body*	14 oz
Sugar (to S.G. 1.090)	
Tannin	$\frac{1}{2}$ tsp
Citric acid	$\frac{1}{8}$ tsp
Malic acid	$\frac{1}{4}$ tsp
Tartaric acid	$\frac{1}{4}$ tsp
Ammonium phosphate	1 tsp
3mg Vitamin B$_1$	1 tablet
Yeast	1 tablet
Lactose	$1\frac{1}{2}$ oz

Social Wines	1 gallon
Sap	
Body*	16 oz
Sugar (to S.G. 1.105)	
Tannin	$\frac{1}{2}$ tsp
Citric acid	$\frac{1}{4}$ tsp
Malic acid	$\frac{1}{2}$ tsp
Tartaric acid	$\frac{1}{2}$ tsp
Ammonium phosphate	1 tsp
3mg Vitamin B$_1$	1 tablet
Yeast	1 tablet
Lactose	2 oz

*Body given as dried fruit weight; this will be one of the grape derivatives (sultanas, raisins, currants), dates or figs. Vegetable, malt, cereal and fresh fruit can also be used in accordance with the previously given table.

Dessert Wines

Sap	1 gallon
Body*	20 oz
Sugar (to S.G. 1.075 in 6 pints)	
Tannin	$\frac{1}{2}$ tsp
Citric acid	$\frac{1}{2}$ tsp
Malic acid	$\frac{3}{4}$ tsp
Tartaric acid	$\frac{3}{4}$ tsp
Ammonium phosphate	1 tsp
3mg Vitamin B_1	1 tablet
Yeast	1 tablet
Lactose	4 oz

*Body given as dried fruit weight; this will be one of the grape derivatives (sultanas, raisins, currants), dates or figs. Vegetable, malt, cereal and fresh fruit can also be used in accordance with the previously given table.

RECIPES

Birch – Sparkling table wine

Ingredients

Birch sap	1 gallon
Pears	12 oz
Sultanas	8 oz
Sugar (to S.G. 1.090)	
Tannin	$\frac{1}{2}$ tsp
Citric acid	$\frac{1}{8}$ tsp
Malic acid	$\frac{1}{4}$ tsp
Tartaric acid	$\frac{1}{4}$ tsp
Ammonium phosphate	1 tsp
3mg Vitamin B$_1$	1 tablet
Yeast, Champagne	1 tablet
Lactose	$1\frac{1}{2}$ oz

Method

Simmer the sap and the peeled pears (diced into half an inch cubes) for fifteen minutes in an aluminium pan, and pour onto the chopped sultanas contained in a sterile plastic bucket. Stir in the acids and the half pint of tea. Allow to cool to 21°C (70°F), keeping covered with a square of linen sheeting. Take a hydrometer reading, and as indicated on the Alcoholic Strength Chart on page 31, stir in the amount of sugar required, dissolved to boiling point in some of the sap and allowed to cool to 21°C. Stir in the ammonium phosphate, the vitamin tablet, and the yeast. Cover with the square of linen sheeting, and

leave for five days at a steady temperature of
21°C, or at a constant room temperature,
stirring twice daily. Strain the liquid through
nylon mesh (a filter bag from a home-
winemaking supplier), into another sterile
bucket, and then syphon into a sterile
fermentation jar, top up to the neck with
boiled and cooled water, if required, and fit
the cork and fermentation lock. Keep at 18°C
(64°F), or at a steady room temperature for a
month, after which, rack and top up, saving
some of the yeast deposit in a small bottle in
the refrigerator. Repeat twice at monthly
intervals, topping up each time. After a total
winemaking time of six months, make a yeast
starter bottle with the refrigerated yeast, and
when it has been fermenting for three days,
syphon the young wine into champagne
bottles, adding a teaspoonful of this starter
and of sugar, together with a proportion of the
lactose, to each bottle before wiring the corks
down. Store at a temperature of about 7–10°C
(45–50°F). After three months, this wine is
ready for drinking. There will be a deposit of
yeast at the bottom (from the starter), and you
can ensure that the wine pours out
sparklingly clear by gradually inverting the
bottles over a period of a few days. Then
freeze the yeast sediment onto the cork, cut
the wire, remove the cork, top up with sugar
syrup, re-cork and re-wire; all this should be
done as expeditiously as possible.

Sycamore – Table wine

Ingredients

Sycamore sap	1 gallon
Raisins	12 oz
Sugar (to S.G. 1.075)	
Tannin	$\frac{1}{2}$ tsp.
Citric acid	$\frac{1}{8}$ tsp.
Malic acid	$\frac{1}{4}$ tsp.
Tartaric acid	$\frac{1}{4}$ tsp.
Ammonium phosphate	1 tsp.
3mg Vitamin B$_1$	1 tablet
Yeast, Graves	1 tablet

Method

Simmer the sap for fifteen minutes in an
aluminium pan, and pour onto the chopped
raisins contained in a sterile plastic bucket.
Stir in the acids and the half pint of tea. Allow
to cool to 21°C (70°F), keeping covered with a
square of linen sheeting. Take a hydrometer
reading, and as indicated on the Alcoholic
Strength Chart, page 31, stir in the
amount of sugar required, dissolved to boiling
point in some of the sap and allowed to cool
to 21°C. Stir in the ammonium phosphate, the
vitamin tablet, and the yeast. Cover with the
square of linen sheeting, and leave for three
days at a steady temperature of 21°C, or at a
constant room temperature, stirring twice
daily. Strain the liquid through nylon mesh
into another sterile bucket, and then syphon
into a sterile fermentation jar, topping up to
the neck with boiled and cooled water, if
required, and fit the cork and fermentation

lock. Keep at 18°C (64°F), or at a steady room
temperature for a month, after which, rack and
top up. Repeat twice at monthly intervals,
topping up each time. After a total
winemaking time of six months, syphon into
bottles or a bulk container, and store at a
temperature of about 7–10°C (45–50°F).

Walnut – Aperitif wine

Ingredients

Walnut sap	1 gallon
Sultanas	14 oz
Sugar (to S.G. 1.105)	
Tannin	$\frac{1}{2}$ tsp
Citric acid	$\frac{1}{4}$ tsp
Malic acid	$\frac{1}{2}$ tsp
Tartaric acid	$\frac{1}{2}$ tsp
Ammonium phosphate	1 tsp
3mg Vitamin B_1	1 tablet
Yeast, Champagne	1 tablet
Lactose	2 oz

Method

Simmer the sap for fifteen minutes in an
aluminium pan, and pour onto the chopped
sultanas contained in a sterile plastic bucket.
Stir in the acids and the half pint of tea. Allow
to cool to 21°C (70°F), keeping covered with a
square of linen sheeting. Take a hydrometer
reading, and as indicated on the Alcoholic
Strength Chart, page 31, stir in the amount
of sugar required, dissolved to boiling
point in some of the sap and allowed to cool
to 21°C. Stir in the ammonium phosphate, the

vitamin tablet, and the crushed yeast tablet.
Cover with the square of linen sheeting, and
leave for seven days at a steady temperature
of 21°C, or at a constant room temperature,
stirring twice daily. Strain the liquid through
nylon mesh into another sterile bucket, and
then syphon into a sterile fermentation jar,
topping up to the neck with boiled and cooled
water, if required, and fit the cork and the
fermentation lock. Keep at 18°C (64°F), or at a
steady room temperature for a month, after
which, rack and top up. Repeat twice at
monthly intervals, topping up each time. After
a total winemaking time of six months, syphon
into bottles or a bulk container, and store at a
temperature of about 7–10°C (45–50°F). Add
the lactose in proportion at decantering time,
stirring it in a little of the wine until it has
dissolved.

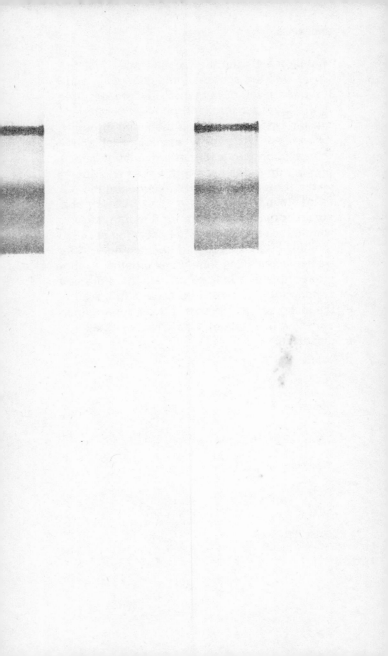

Index of Recipes